eGrade Plus

www.wiley.com/college/huffman
Based on the Activities You Do Every Day

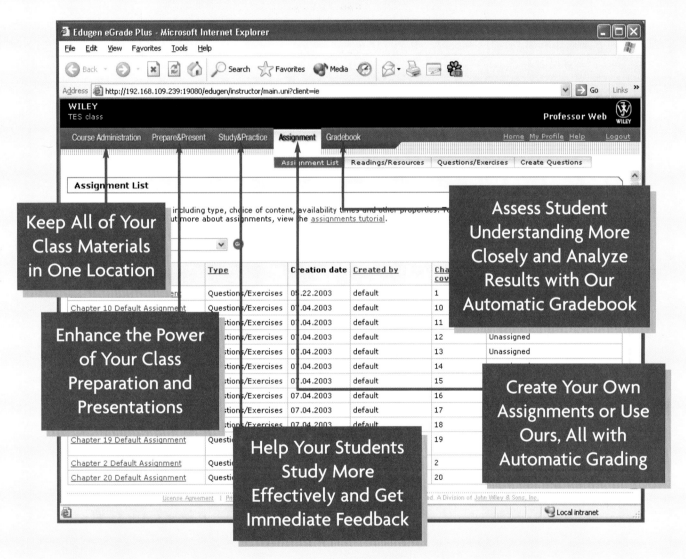

Keep All of Your Class Materials in One Location

Enhance the Power of Your Class Preparation and Presentations

Help Your Students Study More Effectively and Get Immediate Feedback

Assess Student Understanding More Closely and Analyze Results with Our Automatic Gradebook

Create Your Own Assignments or Use Ours, All with Automatic Grading

All the content and tools you need, all in one location, in an easy-to-use browser format.
Choose the resources you need, or rely on the arrangement supplied by us.

Now, many of Wiley's textbooks are available with eGrade Plus, a powerful online tool that provides a completely integrated suite of teaching and learning resources in one easy-to-use website. eGrade Plus integrates Wiley's world-renowned content with media, including a multimedia version of the text, PowerPoint slides, and more. Upon adoption of eGrade Plus, you can begin to customize your course with the resources shown here.

See for yourself!
Go to www.wiley.com/college/egradeplus for an online demonstration of this powerful new software.

Living Psychology

KAREN HUFFMAN *Palomar College*

WILEY

John Wiley & Sons, Inc.

Publisher	Jay O'Callaghan
Editor	Christopher Johnson
Media Editors	Thomas Kulesa/Lynn Pearlman
Assistant Editor	Jessica Bartelt
Marketing Manager	Jeffrey Rucker
Editorial Assistant	Lindsay Lovier
Production Editor	Sandra Dumas
Senior Designer	Kevin Murphy
Senior Illustration Editor	Anna Melhorn
Senior Photo Editor	Sara Wight
Photo Researcher	Elyse Rieder
Production Management Services	Hermitage Publishing Services
Cover and Interior Design	Brian Salisbury
Cover Photo	Diego Rivera, Mexico, Guanajuato, 1886–1957. "Dance in Tehuantepec," 1935 Los Angeles County Museum of Art, Gift of Mr. and Mrs. W. Lipper, from the Milton W. Lipper Estate, M.74.22.4

This book was typeset in 10/12 New Baskerville Roman by Hermitage Publishing Services and printed and bound by Von Hoffmann Corporation. The cover was printed by Von Hoffmann Corporation.

The paper in this book was manufactured by a mill whose forest management programs include sustained yield harvesting of its timberlands. Sustained yield harvesting principles ensure that the number of trees cut each year does not exceed the amount of new growth.

This book is printed on acid-free paper. ∞

Huffman, Karen.
Living Psychology
ISBN-10 0-471-76935-5
ISBN-13 978-0-471-76935-4

Printed in the United States of America.

10 9 8 7 6 5 4 3 2 1

Contents

16

Industrial/Organizational Psychology

(with Gary Piggrem, DeVry University)

Core Learning Outcomes

As you read Chapter 16, keep the following questions in mind and answer them in your own words:

- How has I/O psychology changed from the early 1900s to the present day?

- What are the major concerns of industrial psychologists?

- What does organizational psychology encompass?

Would you like to work at Peet's Coffee and Tea? This California-based company is a large mail-order business, with over 40 retail outlets and more than $42 million in annual sales. The firm pays its workers relatively well and allows full benefits for those who work at least 21 hours a week. Not bad for a company that prides itself on the notion that a paying job shouldn't be confused with having a career. Most employees work part-time at Peet's to earn a living. The flexible hours allow them to pursue special talents in off-job time. Rich Avella is a guitarist, Amie Bailey-Esmont is a doula (a Greek term for someone who helps expectant parents), and Gina Hall is a cross-country mountain bike racer. Like others at Peet's, Rich, Amie, and Gina take pride in being known as "Peetniks."

If Peet's isn't your cup of tea (pun intended), perhaps you would prefer full-time employment. Ben Sawatzky's lumber mill in Edmonton, Canada, won a Pinnacle Award for outstanding entrepreneurship and is considered a prime place to work. A walk-through of his 160-person plant shows why: The plant contains a sauna and gym, and, best of all, there are no supervisors. Instead, employees work in teams with specific production goals. Once these goals are met, they're through for the day. The average workday is 6.75 hours. In addition, employees earn almost double the industry average, along with an annual 10-day paid vacation to Hawaii or Mexico. The company began in 1983 with a personal investment of $1128, a loan of $5000, and two workers. In less than 20 years, sales were more than $60 million. Ben Sawatzky says, "By and large, I haven't run across any other company that has the loyalty of staff we have."

If you don't like working for others, maybe you can start your own business. Dalia Almanza-Smith was quietly enjoying her honeymoon on the beaches of Ibiza, Spain, when she noticed a free picture postcard sponsored by a local restaurant. This innocent act of tourism completely altered her life plans. Dalia recognized the great potential in this simple gimmick. Rather than charging tourists for postcards, she could add a short advertisement and charge the advertiser! Using their savings and credit, Dalia and her husband came up with $40,000 to start their new business. A few years later, their company grew to over $5 million in revenues. Dalia attributes her success partly to being a Hispanic woman—"I learned early to persevere … I was not going to inherit money … I had to invent myself."

(Adapted from Schermerhorn, Hunt, & Osborn, 2000, 2003, pp. 1, 101, 151)

Industrial/Organizational (I/O) Psychology Applied field of psychology concerned with the development and application of scientific principles to the workplace

Whether you're looking for a lifetime of part-time work, full-time employment with great benefits, or owning your own business, the field of industrial/organizational psychology has important information that will help you succeed—at home and work. As you discovered in Chapter 1, psychology is subdivided into many specializations. Some specialities are concerned primarily with the science of psychology (basic research). Others emphasize the application of scientific principles (applied research). **Industrial/organizational (I/O) psychology** is one of the applied fields of psychology concerned with the development and application of scientific principles to the workplace (Spector, 2003).

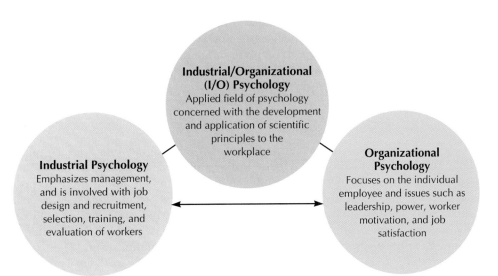

■ FIGURE 16.1 **Specialties within industrial/organizational psychology.** I/O psychology has two major subdivisions, industrial and organizational psychology. Although each division emphasizes different aspects of the workplace, in actual practice their content overlaps and cannot be easily separated.

As its two-part name implies, I/O psychology has two major divisions—industrial and organizational psychology (Figure 16.1). Although the two areas are closely interrelated, **industrial (personnel) psychology** is the older branch, which emphasizes a management perspective. It focuses on job design and employee recruitment, selection, training, and evaluation. In contrast, **organizational psychology** emphasizes the individual employee within the social context of the workplace. It is concerned with such issues as leadership, power, worker motivation, and job satisfaction. This chapter provides an overview of the I/O field and discusses each of the major areas. To set the stage, let's begin with a look at the historical development of I/O psychology.

Industrial (personnel) Psychology Branch of I/O psychology that emphasizes a management perspective

Organizational Psychology Branch of I/O psychology that focuses on the individual employee within the social context of the workplace

◉ MODULE 16.1
The Development of I/O Psychology

The formal study of psychology is relatively short, spanning a mere 125 years or so. The study of I/O psychology is even shorter, originating with the work of Walter Dill Scott, Frederick W. Taylor, and Hugo Munsterberg at the beginning of the twentieth century.

Assessment
How has I/O psychology changed from the early 1900s to the present day?

The Beginnings: Applying Psychology to Sales and Worker Efficiency

On December 20, 1901, Walter Dill Scott, a psychology professor at Northwestern University, addressed a group of advertising professionals. In his talk, he proposed an interesting idea—using psychological principles in the field of advertising. Merely exhibiting a product and hoping that customers would realize their need for it was not enough, Scott thought advertisers could aggressively influence customers by suggesting they buy it or by arguing and debating the undeniable merits of the purchase. In other words, use persuasion and argumentation to sell.

www.wiley.com/college/huffman

Walter Dill Scott

Federick W. Taylor

Hugo Munsterberg

Scott also proposed several other ideas, radical at the time, but taken for granted today. He suggested imitating other companies' successful products, advertising, and production policies; encouraging competition among companies producing similar goods; building loyalty between producers and suppliers; and creating specialized products for markets (Muchinsky, 2002).

Other Major Figures

Frederick W. Taylor, the next major figure in I/O psychology, emphasized the value of designing the work situation to increase worker output. He correctly surmised that if workers performed their jobs more efficiently, the company would increase profits and workers' wages would go up. In his book *The Principles of Scientific Management* (1911), Taylor formulated several principles for increasing the efficiency and profitability of any organization: (1) Scientifically design work methods for greater efficiency; (2) select the best workers and train them in new methods; and (3) encourage cooperation between workers and management to improve the work environment.

A particular story is often told about Taylor's attempt to increase the efficiency of workers who shoveled heavy pig iron. Each man moved an average of 12.5 tons of pig iron per day, which, to most of us, sounds like a lot. However, Taylor allowed the men to rest at scientifically determined periods and designed new shovels to better match the material being moved, which increased each man's output to 47 tons per day! In addition to increased efficiency, Taylor's methods also led to less fatigue and increased wages for the worker and increased profit for the company (Muchinsky, 1993). Taylor was not a psychologist. But he is nevertheless considered one of the founders of human factors psychology—an important subfield of I/O psychology.

Another key historical figure, Hugo Munsterberg, was an early psychologist interested in applying psychology to the workplace. His book *Psychology and Industrial Efficiency* (1913) covered three topics: selecting workers, designing work situations, and using psychology in sales. Munsterberg was most influential in the area of personnel selection and training. His his best known research was a study of streetcar operators, where he created a laboratory simulation of an actual streetcar. This research allowed Munsterberg to develop personnel selection criteria and training procedures that eventually led to better streetcar operators (Muchinsky, 2002).

Scott, Taylor, and Munsterberg all demonstrated the importance of applying psychology in the workplace. However, for many people in industry it took World War I to give I/O psychology real respectability. At the beginning of the war, the American Psychological Association, led by its president, Robert Yerkes, approached Army officials and proposed that psychological testing be used to evaluate the mental ability of recruits. The results could then help establish criteria for assigning recruits to appropriate military jobs.

The Army agreed. Yerkes and a group of psychologists were assigned to develop the first group intelligence test, the *Army Alpha*. Finding that approximately 30 percent of the World War I recruits were functionally illiterate, they later developed the first non-verbal intelligence test, the *Army Beta*.

Walter Dill Scott, mentioned earlier for his advertising ideas, also contributed to the effort to classify and place soldiers in jobs according to their abilities. He is credited with developing job descriptions for over 500 military jobs. Although plans for complete testing of all recruits were never fully implemented, World War I saw a significant expansion of I/O psychology.

The Hawthorne Effect

During the period between World War I and World War II, I/O psychology continued to grow. Many companies added human resource departments for the first time. And a number of colleges and universities began to offer training in I/O psychology. Considerable research also was being conducted on advertising, personnel selection, and

Early I/O psychological tests. Psychologists, led by Robert Yerkes, developed the *Army Alpha,* the first group IQ test. The Army Alpha, and later the *Army Beta,* were used to test and classify World War I recruits.

worker training. But the focus of most I/O research during this period was on testing. Rather than individual testing in the laboratory or in the military, however, workers were now tested in the workplace. In 1924, the most extensive—and by far the most famous—of these workplace projects was begun at the Hawthorne Works of the Western Electric Company, just outside Chicago.

In the original study, researchers from Harvard University installed lights of varying brightness levels in different workrooms where electrical equipment was assembled. The light in some rooms was intense but as subdued as moonlight in others. The object was to study the relationship between worker efficiency and lighting.

The results were quite surprising. Researchers found that worker productivity had little or nothing to do with the lighting level. Productivity improved under both

The Hawthorne effect at work. The Western Electric Hawthorne Works was the site of a famous study of workplace behavior conducted between World War I and World War II.

Would You Like to Conduct Your Own Study on the Hawthorne Effect?

Choose a good friend—let's say your friend is a male—and (without his knowledge) observe him studying or watching television for about five minutes. Write down in detail what he is doing. Document how many times he looks up from his book, changes channels on the television, and so on.

After this period of private observation, ask your friend if you can observe his behavior for five minutes as part of a psychology assignment. Now record the same behaviors. Does his behavior change? Does he look up from his studies more often? Less often? Does he do more or less channel surfing while watching television? If his behavior changes, you may have observed the Hawthorne effect.

Hawthorne Effect Occurs when people change their behavior because of the novelty of the research situation or because they know they are being observed

increased and *decreased* brightness! Even more surprising, when the brightness level remained unchanged, productivity still increased. Simply knowing they were being used as research participants apparently improved worker performance. This is known as the **Hawthorne effect**. People change their behavior because of the novelty of the research situation or because they know they are being observed.

You may have observed the Hawthorne effect in everyday life. When you walk down the sidewalk singing and suddenly notice other people looking at you, you probably stop singing. Similarly, students taking a test are more likely to cheat if they know the professor is not watching. And people are more likely to wash their hands after using a public restroom when others are watching. Little Leaguers also pay more attention to the game when the coach yells their name. In each of these cases, behavior is changed as a result of being observed.

Because of the remarkable findings from the lighting tests, the Hawthorne project was expanded to investigate many other topics, including pre-employment testing, interviewing techniques, and personnel counseling. Various studies continued for over 10 years, ending just as World War II was beginning. The major contribution of the Hawthorne studies was to document the fact that a worker's behavior is influenced not only by the physical setting but also by social factors in the workplace.

Modern Times: Expanding the Role of I/O Psychology

By the beginning of World War II, I/O psychology was an established force in the workplace. Many companies now had personnel offices that routinely tested and placed employees. They also implemented scientifically designed worker-training programs to improve productivity. And researchers were beginning to conduct studies in human factors psychology as machines in the workplace became more complicated.

Many of these advances were applied to the war effort. The first contribution to World War II was the development of the *Army General Classification Test* (AGCT). The AGCT made it possible to classify new recruits into a few broad categories based on their ability to learn the duties and responsibilities of a soldier. I/O psychologists also helped develop tests for selecting and training aircraft pilots and military intelligence agents (spies).

I/O psychology also contributed greatly to the operational safety of airplanes through the design of better control panels. For example, at the beginning of the war many planes and pilots were lost because, when preparing for landing, pilots tended to mistake the landing gear control for the wing flap control. Consequently, pilots tried to land planes with the wheels up or with the wing flaps in the wrong position, providing insufficient lift.

The I/O solution to this problem was simple—design the controls to correspond to their function. The landing gear controls were redesigned to look and feel like wheels and the wing controls were changed to resemble a wing. Following these changes, landing errors were almost completely eliminated! These I/O-inspired World War II airplane design changes are still used on contemporary aircraft.

Another event that helped shape I/O psychology in the United States was the civil rights movement of the late 1950s and early 1960s, which culminated in the Civil Rights Act of 1964. Among other things, it mandated the creation of employment tests, training programs, and recruitment programs that were fair to all job applicants regardless of ethnicity, religion, or gender. Tests given to screen job applicants had to be valid predictors of job performance. For example, general IQ tests could no longer be used to screen applicants at the telephone company for the job of directory assistance operator. Instead, the telephone company might administer a spelling and reading comprehension test.

The Civil Rights Act of 1964 also forced a radical adjustment in corporate recruitment and hiring policies. This change opened many previously unobtainable jobs to ethnic minority and women job applicants. Hence, I/O psychology was now important not only to corporate management but also to the federal government.

I/O psychology and World War II. This photograph of a World War II bomber cockpit shows how human factors psychologists made flying safer and easier. Notice how the controls for the landing gear are designed to look and feel like the function they perform. The landing gear controls are round like a wheel (as shown in box).

Assessment
CHECK & REVIEW

Development of I/O Psychology

Industrial/organizational (I/O) psychology is concerned with the development and application of scientific principles to the workplace. Major founding figures were Walter Dill Scott, Fredrick W. Taylor, and Hugo Munsterberg.

The personnel needs of World War I gave the I/O field respectability. Based on newly developed group IQ tests, Walter Dill Scott developed a program to place recruits in jobs that suited their abilities.

Among important I/O research findings during this period was a phenomenon termed the **Hawthorne effect,** when people change their behavior because of the novelty of a research situation or because they know that they are being observed.

World War II led to scientifically designed worker-training programs to improve productivity for the war effort. The Civil Rights Act of 1964 required I/O psychology to create employment tests, training programs, and recruitment programs that were fair to all job applicants regardless of ethnicity, religion, age, or gender.

Questions
1. Match the founders of I/O psychology (Scott, Taylor, Munsterberg) with their major contribution:

(a) Pioneered methods leading to improved personnel selection and training
(b) Developed principles companies could use to increase worker efficiency and company profit
(c) First to apply psychological principles to advertising

2. Hui-Ching is a consultant who is hired by a large law firm to study worker motivation and job satisfaction. Hui-Ching is part of which branch of I/O psychology? (a) consulting; (b) organizational; (c) personnel; (d) human factors

3. The _____ occurs when research participants change their behaviors because they know they are being observed. (a) halo effect; (b) observational bias; (c) Hawthorne effect; (d) spectator bias

4. How did the Civil Rights Act of 1964 influence I/O psychology?

Answers to Questions can be found at the end of this chapter.

CLICK & REVIEW
for additional assessment options:
www.wiley.com/college/huffman

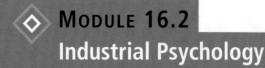

◆ MODULE 16.2
Industrial Psychology

Assessment

What are the major concerns of industrial psychogists?

Now that you've had a brief introduction to the historical background of the entire field of I/O psychology, we can narrow our focus. In this section we will look closely at the industrial part of the field, followed later by a focus on the organizational branch.

This chapter began with a brief description of working conditions at Peet's Coffee and Tea, the lumber mill in Canada, and being your own boss because you need to think carefully about your own career goals. The importance of your career choice cannot be overestimated. During your lifetime you will spend more time at work than at any other single activity—with the possible exception of sleeping. And just as you need an enjoyable career that makes the most of your skills, business and industry need employees who have the right level of skills and motivation to maximize productivity.

Finding "the right person for the right job" is a major component of the industrial branch of I/O psychology. Researchers and practitioners in this field help employers with personnel recruitment, selection, on-the-job training, and performance evaluation. Let's begin with recruitment and selection.

Recruitment and Selection: What Are the Best Methods?

Job Analysis Detailed description of the tasks involved in a job, as well as the knowledge, skills, abilities, and other personal characteristics (KSAOs) an employee must possess to be successful on the job

The first step in finding "the right person" is to carefully define the job itself. A well-done **job analysis** provides information about the tasks involved in a job. It also includes the knowledge, skills, abilities, and other personal characteristics (KSAOs) an employee must possess to be successful on the job. When the job responsibilities and KSAOs are carefully defined and specified in advance, both the applicant and employer can be more efficient in their job search.

Can you imagine what the job analysis would be for a typical college instructor? The knowledge, skills, and abilities necessary to perform as a successful college instructor vary according to academic discipline (psychology, math, physical education, etc.). But all instructors share similar tasks: teaching assigned classes, maintaining required office hours, preparing and grading exams and papers, attending department meetings, and serving on college committees. In addition, many colleges and universities expect professors to conduct research and to publish in professional journals.

If a college wanted to hire a new instructor, it would begin with a job analysis like this, followed by the selection of a large group of candidates. The next step—for any job—is to choose the one most qualified candidate. The number of candidates may be narrowed through applications, questionnaires, interviews, observations, standardized psychological tests, knowledge and skills tests, performance tests, and biodata (detailed biographical information).

Of all these selection devices, the interview continues to be the most popular—and to carry the most weight. Interviews can be *structured* or *unstructured*. Structured interviews involve a set of preplanned questions that are asked of every person who is interviewed and a standardized rating of the applicant's qualifications. This reduces several biases associated with unstructured interviews, which tend to be casual, short, and made up of random questions. As expected, structured interviews are generally better predictors of job performance than unstructured interviews (Hermelin & Robertson, 2001; Huffcutt, Conway, Roth, & Stone, 2001; Moscoso, 2000).

If you are asked to come in for an interview, it may be either structured or unstructured. But you can expect a face-to-face meeting with one or more interviewers who are using the interview as an alternative or adjunct to the application form. Their questions are designed to measure your attitudes ("Did you like your last job?" "Do you pre-

TABLE 16.1 WHY MOST PEOPLE DISLIKE INTERVIEWS

Problems:

"First date" syndrome	In initial meetings with important, but unstated, outcomes, both parties behave with artificial care and skill.
Nervousness	Applicants know they are being evaluated and compared to others, and they are typically in a "one-down" position (they need what the employer has to give). Thus, most interviewees are tense and anxious.
Subjectivity	When one person meets another, impressions tend to be formed immediately—sometimes due to nothing more than clothes or facial appearance. These first impressions are often resistant to change.

Source: Auerbach, 1996

fer working in groups or alone?"), job experiences ("What did you do in your last job?"), and personal background ("What was your college major?"). Interviewers also use this face-to-face meeting to assess your communication and interpersonal skills. Successful applicants are typically friendly (but not overly so), eager (but not desperate), and assertive (but not aggressive).

Is interviewing really that complicated? I'm getting nervous just reading about this. Most interviewees tend to be anxious, and that is perfectly normal (Table 16.1). But there are also reasons to look forward to interviews. First, interviews allow for longer and more detailed answers than application forms, and most people find it easier to talk than to write. In addition, both parties have the opportunity to ask questions and to clarify exactly what the job requires. In effect, you are interviewing the company as much as it is interviewing you.

Application
TRY THIS YOURSELF

Interviewer Versus Interviewee

If you would like to improve your interviewing skills, try the following:

1. **Research.** Before your interview, research the company, employer, supervisors, and the knowledge, skills, abilities, and other personal characteristics (KSAOs) required for the advertised position. The information you gather can be invaluable in helping you respond to interview questions. Also, simply knowing the history and size of the company will show the interviewer that you are serious about your job search. Research can also help you decide if you really want to work for this company.

2. **Role-playing.** Ask someone to help you practice playing both interviewer and interviewee. Encourage honest feedback about your verbal and nonverbal habits that may affect your interview. For example, do you nervously jiggle your feet or avoid eye contact?

Also, brainstorm ahead of time about potential questions and good responses.

3. **Personality.** As mentioned before, interviewers generally like friendly, eager, and assertive applicants. These are basic personality traits you've undoubtedly displayed before—when meeting new friends or on a first date, for example. Recognizing that you've used these skills in the past may help you relax in the interview—and be yourself.

(On the other hand, if you become an interviewer, you can make the interview process more comfortable—and therefore more productive—in several ways. Most important, recognize that the applicant is tense. Begin by introducing yourself. Be relaxed and friendly, and briefly describe what the interview will be like. Tell how long it will take and what topics will be discussed. Finally, encourage the interviewee to ask questions.)

www.wiley.com/college/huffman

Employee Training: Objectives and Methods

After applicants are tested and interviewed and the best candidate is hired, the I/O psychologist may help train the new employee. Research shows that training provides workers with appropriate skills for the assigned job. It also reduces frustration and stress (Kaul, 2002; Muchinsky, 2002).

Training typically begins with some form of orientation. Just as you may have had a college orientation designed to introduce the educational organization, new employees are usually given either a formal or informal introduction to the business setting. Pay close attention. The orientation is designed to "clue in" new employees. You are being taught the facts of organizational structure and operations as well as appropriate attitudes and allegiances.

Organizational Culture A group's shared pattern of thought and action; a common perception held by the organization's members

Every organization has its shared pattern of thought and action, an **organizational culture**. This culture arises from each group's history and involves group identity, policies, and rituals. Organizations typically develop characteristic attitudes toward diversity, creativity, attention to detail, team versus individual orientation, and stability versus innovation (Hurley & Hult, 1998; Koslowsky, Sagie, & Stashevsky, 2002; Mor, Barak, & Leuin, 2002). Fitting into an organization means fitting into its culture.

I/O psychologists are also involved with training and upgrading skills for new and existing employees. Skills training can be technical and highly job specific. You might be taught how to sell or service the company's product, or how to operate the communication system and other machines. General training may also be offered for interpersonal skills, including effective listening, communication, and how to be a "team player."

Evaluating Workers: Measuring Job Performance

Performance Evaluation Formal procedure used by an organization to assess employee job performance

After an employee has been recruited, selected, trained, and worked at the job for a time, his or her performance is then evaluated. **Performance evaluation** is the formal procedure an organization uses to assess the multidimensional job performance of employees (Arvey & Murphy, 1998). Organizations use performance evaluations for a number of purposes. One of the most important is providing feedback to the employee on how the organization views his or her performance. Employees need to know when they are doing well (so they can keep on doing well) and when they are not (so they can change). Research shows that employees fare better when their work is evaluated, when reinforcers are closely related to job performance, and when criticism is delivered constructively (Baron, 1990; Johnson & Helgeson, 2002).

Performance evaluations also are useful for identifying training and development needs. Does the employee need upgrading of skills or retraining? In addition, management uses performance evaluations for decisions on promotions, transfers, and termination.

A performance evaluation may be *objective* or *subjective*. Objective measures include such things as the amount of sales for a salesperson or the number of publications for a college instructor. Many jobs (like management and support services), however, do not have an easily identifiable and objective product. And in some cases objective measures may not be appropriate. For example, how do you identify the *product* of a college instructor's teaching? The effect of one college instructor on any one student's learning is difficult to measure objectively. Furthermore, benefits from a college instructor or a college degree are sometimes not apparent until a future time.

Subjective measures avoid some of these problems (but introduce others, as you will shortly see). Subjective ratings by supervisors or others who are familiar with the employee's job performance are the most common form of performance evaluation.

For example, college instructors are frequently evaluated by students in their classes or peers in their department.

Despite their popularity, subjective methods suffer from serious rater biases and other human errors (Arvey & Murphy, 1998). One of the most widely researched problems is the tendency to rate individuals either too high or too low based on one outstanding trait, the **halo error**. If a person is rated "exceptional" in one area, he or she tends to be rated "exceptional" in all areas. The same thing occurs when someone is rated "poor" in one area.

Halo Error Tendency to rate individuals either too high or too low based on one outstanding trait

The halo error is a significant problem. If a supervisor happens to value friendliness, will he or she overrate an employee who smiles a lot? Also, how can we differentiate between what might be termed a *legitimate halo*—an employee who does perform well on all dimensions—and bias caused by the undue influence of one characteristic? How to prevent or minimize the halo error is a major research topic in personnel psychology (Baltes & Parker, 2000; Hoyt, 2000; Li, Wang, & Zhang, 2002).

To offset problems with the halo error and other evaluation biases, some organizations have recently turned to "360-degree" performance measures. These measures include evaluations from supervisors, peers, subordinates, and even customers. Multisource measures are also useful for both feedback and personnel decisions.

In addition, organizations may use specially designed rating scales, where the supervisor evaluates an employee in certain critical areas by assigning a numerical rating. As Figure 16.2 shows, your job as a student could be evaluated with this type of rating scale. The idea is that raters will be more accurate if they focus on specific behaviors rather than traits, such as friendliness.

Although rating scales are helpful, they also have drawbacks. As you know, some college instructors can be hard graders, while others may be easy. Supervisors in the work world can be similarly tough or lenient raters. In addition, research shows that supervisors do, in fact, give higher ratings to employees they like (Ferris et al., 1994).

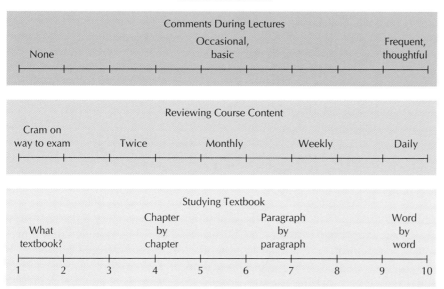

■ **FIGURE 16.2   A possible rating scale for students.** How would you score on this rating scale? Would you like this kind of performance evaluation, or do you prefer the traditional rating scale, known as "grades"?

www.wiley.com/college/huffman

Assessment
CHECK & REVIEW

◇ Industrial Psychology

The industrial branch of I/O psychology is concerned with recruiting, selecting, training, and evaluating workers. Recruitment begins with a **job analysis,** a detailed description of the tasks involved in a job, as well as the KSAOs an employee must possess to be successful on the job. Interviews are the most popular method of selection, and structured interviews are better predictors of job performance than unstructured interviews. Employee training typically begins with an orientation program. One of the major unstated goals of orientation is transmitting the **organizational culture**—the group's shared patterns of thought and action.

Performance evaluation is the formal procedure an organization uses to assess the job performance of employees. These evaluations can be objective or subjective. The subjective method is the most popular, but its efficiency is lessened by the **halo error** (the tendency to rate individuals too high or too low based on one outstanding trait). To offset the halo error, some organiza-

tions use 360-degree multisource measures and special rating scales.

Questions
1. What are the three basic personality traits that most appeal to interviewers?
2. If an employer used the number of cases won by a lawyer as part of his or her performance evaluation, this would be an example of _____. (a) the halo error; (b) an objective measure; (c) a 360-degree mulitsource measure; (d) a subjective measure
3. What are the two major functions of performance evaluations?

Answers to Questions can be found at the end of this chapter.

CLICK & REVIEW
for additional assessment options:
www.wiley.com/college/huffman

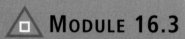

▣ MODULE 16.3
Organizational Psychology

When it comes to work, most people are social animals—they generally prefer to work with others. *Organizational psychology* focuses on the individual employee within the social context of the workplace. In this section, we discuss two topics of special interest to organizational psychologists—worker motivation and job satisfaction.

Worker Motivation: Goal-Setting, Equity, and Expectancy

Assessment

What does organizational psychology encompass?

Why do some workers put in long hours even when they are not being directly compensated? Why do others arrive late, do the minimum, and leave early if the boss isn't looking? You may have some answers after having read about personality differences and motivation and reinforcement in earlier chapters of this book (e.g., Chapters 6, 10, 11, and 14). In this section, we will explore three theories I/O psychologists have developed about what motivates workers: *goal-setting theory, equity theory,* and *expectancy theory.*

Goal-Setting Theory

When you read about business owner Dalia Almanza-Smith at the beginning of the chapter, did you admire her and wonder what it takes to gain her level of success? Like other college professors, your authors have repeatedly noticed that our students who are most likely to succeed are not necessarily the ones with the highest IQ scores. The highest achievers generally have challenging, specific, and well-defined goals for what they want out of their college education compared to our students with less focused general goals, such as "to get a degree."

Researchers have supported what we've observed in our students. According to **goal-setting theory** (Bandura & Locke, 2003; Locke, 1968, 2000; Locke & Latham, 1990, 2002), setting specific and difficult (but attainable) goals leads to higher performance. A *goal* is defined as whatever a person consciously wants to obtain or achieve. Locke and Henne (1986) have identified four ways goals affect people's behavior: They focus attention and action on goal-related behaviors, motivate people to try harder, increase persistence, and encourage individuals to search for effective strategies to attain their goals.

Goal-setting theory has been widely studied and is strongly supported by research evidence (e.g., Ammerman et al., 2002; Gilbourne & Taylor, 1998; Latham, 2001; Zetik & Stuhlmacher, 2002). It is currently the most popular theory of motivation in industrial/organizational psychology (Spector, 2003). However, researchers also have noted several drawbacks to goal setting. For example, workers sometimes focus so much on their goals that they ignore other equally important job requirements. And goals occasionally conflict, so that working on one prevents working on another (Ambrose & Kulik, 1999).

Equity Theory

In contrast to goal-setting theory, **equity theory** suggests we are strongly motivated to maintain a sense of equilibrium or balance in our dealings with others and with organizations. At work, we prefer jobs in which the output is equal to the input. If imbalance occurs, we will adjust our input, output, or psychological perceptions (Beckett-Camarata et al., 1998; Duncan, 2001; Kulik, 2002; van Dierendonck, Schaufeli, & Buunk, 2001).

According to equity theory, in our search for balance, we begin by comparing our contributions, job rewards, and compensations to that of our coworkers, friends, neighbors, and colleagues in other organizations. If we perceive that our *job input* (contributions) matches our *job outcome* (rewards), we are happy because there is a state of balance or *equity*. On the other hand, if we detect an imbalance (we're giving more than we're getting in return), we may adjust our input (by decreasing our efforts or quitting). We also may try to increase our output (by asking for more pay or other compensations). Or we can adjust our perceptions (by focusing on other compensations, such as time off, ease of work, and work friendships).

It is important to note that *actual* equity is less important than *perceived* equity. As a supervisor, you may have overwhelming objective evidence that workers are being treated equitably. If your employees perceive that they are being shortchanged, however, they may decrease their input, increase their requests for output, or adjust their perceptions. Obviously, it is important for supervisors to communicate effectively with employees and to discover how they perceive the situation.

As you can see, a perception of equity is important but it can be difficult to achieve and maintain. Huseman and Hatfield (1989) have offered three explanations for these difficulties:

1. **Wrong psychological currency.** We tend to give people what we would like to get, or what we think they want, rather than what they really want. For example, supervisors may give their employees more money despite repeated requests for more job flexibility. This can leave both supervisors and workers feeling frustrated and resentful.
2. **Trust bankruptcy.** Many workers (and children and lovers) do not trust others because they've been "burned" by broken promises in the past.

"Oh, not bad. The light comes on, I press the bar, they write me a check. How about you?"

© The New Yorker Collection (1993) Tom Cheney from Cartoonbank.com.

Goal-Setting Theory Having specific and difficult, but attainable, goals leads to higher performance

Equity Theory Individuals need a sense of balance where output is equal to input

www.wiley.com/college/huffman

A Test for Equity

Are you an employer, parent, or lover who wants to increase the perceived equity in your relations with others? Try Huseman and Hatfield's (1989) five-step model, the *equity power paradigm*.

• *Perspective.* Work to understand the perceptions of others and to communicate your own perspective before problems arise.

• *Positive expectations.* Let others know that you have high expectations and confidence in them.
• *Goal setting.* Provide specific, challenging, but attainable goals.
• *Performance feedback.* Offer regular evaluation and feedback—especially constructive, positive suggestions.
• *Rewards.* Provide important and frequent rewards for appropriate behaviors.

---

3. **Hidden expectations.** We often have unspoken, or poorly communicated, desires and expectations. Unfortunately, we still expect others to "read our minds" and satisfy these hidden expectations. As you may recall from Chapter 10, these poorly understood and unrealistic demands can wreak havoc on marital and family relationships. This also is true in the workplace.

Expectancy Theory

Expectancy Theory Expectancy of outcomes, their desirability, and the effort needed to achieve them all determine worker motivation

One of the oldest and most popular theories of worker motivation is Vroom's (1964) **expectancy theory**. This theory suggests workers perform in line with their expectancy of outcomes, the desirability of those outcomes, and the effort needed to achieve them. Before deciding to work hard (or not to work hard), individuals reportedly ask themselves three questions:

1. *What can I reasonably expect from my efforts?* If employees perceive that rewards such as salary increases, bonuses, and promotions are based on hard work, they will work hard. If workers believe rewards are based on factors such as seniority or politics, both motivation and morale will be extremely low.
2. *Do I really want the rewards offered by management?* If you've been working hard hoping for a salary increase but are offered a promotion with increased responsibility and only a small bonus, you will obviously be disappointed. Similarly, if you had put in long hours hoping for a transfer to the West Coast office but instead were offered the East Coast, you would be very disappointed. Managers should recognize that individual workers have different ideas of what is rewarding.
3. *If I give maximum effort, will it be reflected in my job evaluation?* For some employees, the answer is too often no. If you lack the training or necessary skill level for a particular job, you are unlikely to be a high performer, no matter how hard you try. On the other hand, some workers are qualified but their supervisors may be unfair or may not like them. Regardless of their efforts, these external situations may block them from getting a good evaluation.

In sum, general knowledge of the three major worker motivation theories (goal setting, equity, and expectancy) and implementation of this knowledge can help improve your own job performance and your management of others.

Job Satisfaction: What Are the Important Factors?

What is the worst job you have ever had? What made it so bad? Was it the working conditions or low pay? Perhaps it was the work itself. Or maybe you just hated sitting at a desk for eight hours. Job satisfaction research is a high priority for I/O psychologists.

In this section, we examine why managers should be concerned about employee job satisfaction (benefits to management and employees) and what factors determine worker satisfaction (personality/job factors).

Benefits to Management and Employees

Workers obviously prefer jobs that are rewarding and satisfying. But why should managers or business owners care if their employees are satisfied or not? According to research, there are several reasons (Griffeth & Gaertner, 2001; Kinzel & Nanson, 2000; Murphy & Athanasou, 2002; Sanders, 2001; Stein, 2001; Vagg, Spielberger, & Wasala, 2002; Zboril-Benson, 2002):

1. *Decreased absenteeism and resignations.* Dissatisfied workers are more likely to resign or be absent from work, which is one of the highest expenses for employers.

2. *Improved employee health.* Job satisfaction carries over to the employee's life inside and outside the office—*the spillover hypothesis.* Studies show that satisfied workers have less stress, less burnout, and better physical and psychological health. In fact, job satisfaction may be a better predictor of length of life than physical condition or tobacco use.

3. *Increased productivity.* Research shows that job satisfaction almost always leads to increased productivity. Most of us think of productivity in terms of increased sales or production. But job satisfaction also affects productivity through increased *organizational citizenship behavior* (OCB). OCB is generally defined as behavior that goes beyond the formal requirements of the job and is beneficial to the organization. Examples would be helping another employee or supervisor (even when it is not required), making innovative suggestions for improvement, and punctuality.

"All work and no play makes you a valued employee."

Personality/Job Factors

Now that we know that job satisfaction is important to both employer and employee, how do we discover what determines job satisfaction? One of the most interesting and influential answers comes from John Holland (1985, 1994). According to Holland's

Application
TRY THIS YOURSELF

Increasing Worker Motivation

If you are a manager interested in increasing worker motivation, here are three ways you (and your employees) can benefit from expectancy theory:

- *Clarify the route to rewards.* Be sure that promotions, salary increases, and bonuses are based on clear, definable measures of performance. Communicate these measures to your employees and give them frequent feedback on their efforts.
- *Personalize the payoffs.* Ensure the rewards you've chosen for good performance are meaningful or valued by your employees. Ask employees to help design payoffs that fit their personal goals and expectations.
- *Reward maximum effort.* Begin by establishing a good fit between employees and their job assignments, and then ensure that employees are well trained. Once they are established in the work position, provide employees frequent evaluation on their work, including feedback on how their current performance level will affect their long-term job promotions and raises.

Personality–Job Fit Theory
Identifies six personality types and proposes that a good fit between these personality types and occupations helps determine job satisfaction

personality–job fit theory, a match (or "good fit") between a person's personality and occupation is a major factor in job satisfaction.

Holland developed a *Self-Directed Search* questionnaire that scores people on six personality types and then matches them with various occupations. By matching personality types to appropriate occupations, Holland believes workers will bring the right interests and abilities to a job's demands. This "good-fit" match between personality and occupation ensures success on the job and a higher level of job satisfaction (people tend to like what they are good at). Studies generally support Holland's theory (Brkich, Jeffs, & Carless, 2002; Furnham, 2001; Spokane, Meir, & Catalano, 2000; Tett & Murphy, 2002).

Assessment
CHECK & REVIEW

▲ Organizational Psychology

Organizational psychology focuses on the individual employee within the social context of the workplace. **Goal-setting theory** suggests that having specific and difficult goals improves performance. **Equity theory** says workers are motivated if they perceive that their job inputs match the perceived rewards. **Expectancy theory**, on the other hand, maintains that employees are motivated to work according to their expectancy of outcomes, the desirability of those outcomes, and the effort needed to achieve them.

Job satisfaction is important to both employer and employee. Employers gain because they save money (lower absenteeism and fewer resignations) and increase productivity. Employees gain because they are under less stress, enjoy better physical health, and have an improved overall quality and length of life.

According to **personality–job fit theory**, job satisfaction results from a match between personality and occupation. Supportive colleagues, supportive working conditions, mentally challenging work, and equitable rewards are also important.

Questions

1. Identify the worker motivation theory that best explains the following situations:
   (a) Seong enjoys assignments that are difficult but attainable.
   (b) Denise avoids work and responsibility but does not fear being fired because she is best friends with the boss and enjoys high seniority.
   (c) Juan, a salaried employee, feels he is being underpaid so he decides to cut back on his hours at work.
2. How does management benefit when employees have job satisfaction? What are the major benefits of job satisfaction to employees?
3. The theory that a match between a person's personality and occupation results in increased job satisfaction is known as_____. (a) expectancy theory; (b) the halo effect; (c) participative decision making; (d) personality–job fit theory

Answers to Questions can be found at the end of this chapter.

CLICK & REVIEW
for additional assessment options:
www.wiley.com/college/huffman

Assessment

Key Terms

*To assess your understanding of the **Key Terms** in Chapter 16, write a definition for each (in your own words), and then compare your definitions with those in the text.*

Achievement
Web Sources

Huffman Book Companion Site

http://www.wiley.com/college/huffman

This site is loaded with free Interactive Self-Tests, Internet Exercises, Glossary and Flashcards for key terms, web links, Handbook for Non-Native Speakers, and other activities designed to improve your mastery of the material in this chapter.

Want more information on the general field of I/O psychology?

http://www.siop.org/

This richly layered home page of the Society for Industrial and Organizational Psychology, Inc. contains numerous links to Internet resources, services, careers in I/O psychology, member information, and more.

Want even more general information?

http://www.sosig.ac.uk/roads/subject-listing/World/indpsych.html

Sponsored by the Social Science Information Gateway, this website is another great starting place for information about the field. As you'll notice on the opening page, this is one of the largest I/O psychology database on the Internet. In these pages, you'll find links to conferences, courses, and other invaluable sources of information.

Would you like an Internet survival guide for I/O psychology?

http://allserv.rug.ac.be/~flievens/guide.htm

As stated on its home page, "This guide provides a plethora of Internet sites valuable to both practitioners and researchers in the field of Industrial and Organizational Psychology. The contents of the survival guide are regularly updated. The intention was to list interesting Internet resources for the following four topics: Human Resource Management, Organizational Psychology, Statistics, and Methodology.

Interested in human factors?

http://human-factors.arc.nasa.gov/

The stated NASA mission for this site is to develop a world-class center for human factors research and to promote the broadest possible application of this research.

Want another interesting site dedicated to human factors?

http://ergo.human.cornell.edu/

Sponsored by Cornell's Human Factors and Ergonomics Program, this website focuses on methods to improve comfort, performance, and health through the ergonomic design of products and environments.

Answers to Review Questions

Development of I/O Psychology Page 633 (a) Munsterberg, (b) Taylor, (c) Scott. 2. b. 3. c. 4. The Civil Rights Act of 1964 forced I/O psychologists to make tests and procedures valid for all workers, not just the white majority. *Industrial Psychology Page 638* 1. Friendliness, eagerness, and assertiveness. 2. b. 3. The two major functions are to provide feedback to the employee on his or her performance and to identify training or development needs. *Organizational Psychology Page 642* 1. a. (goal-setting); b. (expectancy); c. (equity). 2. Management benefits from employee job satisfaction because there are fewer resignations, less absenteeism, and improved overall productivity. Employees benefit because they have less stress, better health, and improved overall quality of life. 3. d.

Visual Summary

◻ The Development of I/O Psychology

The Beginnings → **Modern Times**

Major Figures: Scott, Taylor and Munsterberg.	World War I: I/O psychology gained respectability and the **Hawthorne Effect** was identified.	World War II: I/O psychology developed worker training programs.	Civil Rights Act of 1964: I/O psychology created bias free tests and programs.

Industrial/Organizational (I/O) Psychology
Applied field of psychology concerned with the development and application of scientific principles to the workplace

Industrial Psychology
Emphasizes management, and is involved with job design and recruitment, selection, training, and evaluation of workers

Organizational Psychology
Focuses on the individual employee and issues such as leadership, power, worker motivation, and job satisfaction

◇ Industrial Psychology

Recruitment and Selection → **Employee Training** → **Evaluating Workers**

Begins with a **job analysis** describing job tasks and employee required knowledge, skills, abilities, and other personal characteristics (KSAOs).	Begins with an orientation where the **organizational culture** is transmitted.	Subjective evaluations are more popular than objective ones, but they may experience **halo error**.

Worker Motivation

What motivates employees?

Goal Setting Theory suggests specific and difficult (but attainable) goals improve performance.

Equity Theory believes individuals need a sense of balance where output is equal to input.

Expectancy Theory suggests expectancy of outcomes, their desirability, and the effort needed to achieve them all affect worker motivation.

Worker Motivation

Why is job satisfaction important?
- Employers gain because they save money (through lower absenteeism and fewer resignations) and increase worker productivity.
- Employees enjoy better physical health, less stress, and improved overall quality of life.

References

Ambrose, M. L., & Kulik, C. T. (1999). Old friends, new faces: Motivation research in the 1990s. *Journal of Management, 25*(3), 231-292.

Ammerman, A. S., Lindquist, C. H., Lohr, K. N., & Hersey, J. (2002). The efficacy of behavioral interventions to modify dietary fat and fruit and vegetable intake: A review of the evidence. *Preventive Medicine: An International Journal Devoted to Practice & Theory, 35*(1), 25-41.

Arvey, R. D., & Murphy, K. R. (1998). Performance evaluation in work settings. *Annual Review of Psychology, 49,* 141-168.

Baltes, B. B., & Parker, C. P. (2000). Reducing the effects of performance expectations on behavioral ratings. *Organizational Behavior & Human Decision Processes, 82*(2), 237-267.

Bandura, A., & Locke, E. A. (2003). Negative self-efficacy and goal effects revisited. *Journal of Applied Psychology, 88*(1), 87-99.

Baron, R. A. (1990). Countering the effect of destructive criticism: The relative efficacy of four interventions. *Journal of Applied Psychology, 75,* 235-245.

Beckett-Camarata, E. J., Camarata, M. R., & Barker, R. T. (1998). Integrating internal and external customer relationships through relationship management: A strategic response to a changing global environment. *Journal of Business Research, 41*(1), 71-81.

Brkich, M., Jeffs, D., & Carless, S. A. (2002). A global self-report measure of person-job fit. *European Journal of Psychological Assessment, 18*(1), 43-51.

Duncan, W. J. (2001). Stock ownership and work. *Organizational Dynamics, 30*(1), 1-11.

Ferris, G. R., Judge, T. A., Rowland, K. M., & Fitzgibbons, D. E. (1994). Subordinate influence and the performance evaluation process: Test of a model. *Organizational and Human Decision Processes, 58,* 101-135.

Furnham, A. (2001). Vocational preference and P-O fit: Reflections on Holland's theory of vocational choice. *Applied Psychology: An International Review, 50*(1), 5-29.

Gilbourne, D. & Taylor, A. H. (1998). From theory to practice: The integration of goal perspective theory and life development approaches within an injury-specific goal-setting program. *Journal of Applied Sport Psychology, 10*(1), 124-139.

Griffeth, R. W., & Gaertner, S. (2001). A role for equity theory in the turnover process: An empirical test. *Journal of Applied Social Psychology, 31*(5), 1017-1037.

Hermelin, E., & Robertson, I. T. (2001). A critique and standardization of meta-analytic validity coefficients in personnel selection. *Journal of Occupational & Organizational Psychology, 74*(3), 253-277.

Holland, J. L. (1985). *Making vocational choices: A theory of vocational personalities and work environments* (2nd ed). Englewood Cliffs, NJ: Prentice Hall.

Holland, J. L. (1994). *Self-directed search form.* R. Lutz, Fl: Psychological Assessment Resources.

Hoyt, W. T. (2000). Rater bias in psychological research: When is it a problem and what can we do about it? *Psychological Methods, 5*(1), 64-86.

Huffcutt, A. I., Conway, J. M., Roth, P. L., & Stone, N. J. (2001). Identification and meta-analytic assessment of psychological constructs measured in employment interviews. *Journal of Applied Psychology, 86*(5), 897-913.

Hurley, R. F., & Hult, G. T. M. (1998). Innovation, market orientation, and organizational learning: An integration and empirical examination. *Journal of Marketing, 62*(3), 42-54.

Huseman, R. C., & Hatfield, J. D. (1989). *Managing the equity factor...or "After all I've done for you..."* Boston: Houghton-Mifflin.

Johnson, M., & Helgeson, V. S. (2002). Sex differences in response to evaluative feedback: A field study. *Psychology of Women Quarterly, 26*(3), 242-251.

Kaul, R. E. (2002). A social worker's account of 31 days responding to the Pentagon disaster: Crisis intervention training and self-care practices. *Brief Treatment & Crisis Intervention, 2*(1), 33-37.

Kinzel, A., & Nanson, J. (2000). Education and debriefing: Strategies for preventing crises in crisis-line volunteers. *Crisis, 21*(3), 26-134.

Koslowsky, M., Sagie, A., & Stashevsky, S. (2002). Introduction: Cultural relativism and universalism in organizational behaviors. *International Journal of Cross Cultural Management, 2*(2), 131-135.

Kulik, L. (2002). Marital equality and the quality of long-term marriage in later life. *Ageing & Society, 22*(4), 459-481.

Latham, G. P. (2001). The reciprocal effects of science on practice: Insights from the practice and science of goal setting. *Canadian Psychology, 42*(1), 1-11.

Li, F., Wang, E., & Zhang, F. (2002). The multitrait-multirater approach to analyzing rating biases. *Acta Psychologica Sinica, 34*(1), 89-96.

Locke, E. A. (1968). Toward a theory of task motivation and performance. *Organizational Behavior and Human Performance, 4,* 309-329.

Locke, E. A. (2000). Motivation, cognition, and action: An analysis of studies of task goals and knowledge. *Applied Psychology: An International Review, 49,* 408-429.

Locke, E. A., & Henne, D. (1986). Work motivation theories. In C. L. Cooper & I. T. Robertson (Eds.), *International review of industrial and organizational psychology* (pp. 1-35). Chichester, UK: John Wiley.

Locke, E. A., & Latham, G. P. (1990). *A theory of goal setting & task performance.* Englewood Cliffs, NJ: Prentice Hall.

Locke, E. A., & Latham, G. P. (2002). Building a practically useful theory of goal setting and task motivation: A 35-year odyssey. *American Psychologist, 57*(9), 705-717.

Mor, Barak, M., & Leuin, A. (2002). Outside of the corporate mainstream and excluded from the work community: A study of diversity, job satisfaction and well-being. *Community, Work & Family, 5*(2), 133-157.

Moscoso, S. (2000). A review of validity evidence, adverse impact and applicant reactions. *International Journal of Selection & Assessment, 8*(4), 237-247.

Muchinksky, P. M. (1993). *Psychology applied to work* (4th ed.). Pacific Grove, CA: Brooks Cole.

Muchinsky, P. M. (2002). *Psychology applied to work: An introduction to industrial and organizational psychology* (7th ed.). Pacific Grove, CA: Wadsworth.

Murphy, G., & Athanasou, J. (2002). Job satisfaction and organizational citizenship behaviour: A study of Australian human-service professionals. *Journal of Managerial Psychology, 17*(4), 287-297.

Sanders, M. A. (2001). Minimizing stress in the workplace: Whose responsibility is it? *Work: Journal of Prevention, Assessment & Rehabilitation, 17*(3), 263-165.

Schermerhorn, J. R., Hunt, J. G., & Osborn, R. N. (2003). *Organizational behavior* (8th ed.). New York, Wiley.

Spector, P. E. (2003). *Industrial organizational psychology: Research and practice* (3rd ed.). New York: Wiley.

Spokane, A. R., Meir, E. I., & Catalano, M. (2000). Person-environment congruence and Holland's theory: A review and reconsideration. *Journal of Vocational Behavior, 57*(2), 137-187.

Stein, F. (2001). Occupational stress, relaxation therapies, exercise and biofeedback. *Work: Journal of Prevention, Assessment & Rehabilitation, 17*(3), 235-246.

Taylor, F. W. (1911). *The principles of scientific management.* New York: Harper.

Tett, R. P., & Murphy, P. J. (2002). Personality and situations in co-worker preference: Similarity and complementarity in worker compatibility. *Journal of Business & Psychology, 17*(2), 223-243.

Vagg, P. R., Spielberger, C. D., & Wasala, C. F. (2002). Effects of organizational level and gender on stress in the workplace. *International Journal of Stress Management, 9*(4), 243-261.

van Dierendonck, D., Schaufeli, W. B., & Buunk, B. P. (2001). Burnout and inequity among human service professionals: A longitudinal study. *Journal of Occupational Health Psychology, 6*(1), 43-52.

Vroom, V. (1964). *Work and motivation.* New York: Wiley.

Zboril-Benson, L. R. (2002). Why nurses are calling in sick: The impact of health-care restructuring. *Canadian Journal of Nursing Research/Revue canadienne de recherche en sciences infirmieres, 33*(4), 89-107.

Zetik, D. C., & Stuhlmacher, A. F. (2002). Goal setting and negotiation performance: A meta-analysis. *Group Processes & Intergroup Relations, 5*(1), 35-52.

Photo Credits

Index

HISTORY OF PSYCHOLOGY TIMELINE FROM 1859 TO 1992

▷ 1859

Charles Darwin

Publishes *On the Origin of Species*, in which he outlines his highly influential theory of evolution through natural selection.

▷ 1879

Wilhelm Wundt

Creates the first psychology laboratory at the University of Leipzig in Germany, publishes the first psychology text, *Principles of Physiological Psychology*, and is considered the founder of experimental psychology.

▷ 1882

G. Stanley Hall

Receives first American Ph.D. in psychology, establishes what some consider the first American Psychology lab at Johns Hopkins University, and later founds the American Psychological Association.

▷ 1890

William James

Writes *The Principles of Psychology*, in which he promotes his psychological ideas that are later grouped together under the term functionalism.

▷ 1900

Sigmund Freud

Publishes *Interpretation of Dreams* and presents his ideas on psychoanalysis, which later became a very influential form of psychotherapy and theory of personality.

▷ 1905

Alfred Binet

Develops the first intelligence test in France. Lewis Terman later published the Stanford-Binet Intelligence Scale, which becomes the world's foremost intelligence test.

▷ 1906

Ivan Pavlov

Publishes his learning research on the salivation response in dogs, which later became known as classical conditioning.

▷ 1913

John Watson

Publishes his article *"Psychology as the Behaviorist Views It,"* in which he describes the science of behaviorism.

▷ 1925

Wolfgang Kohler

Publishes *The Mentality of Apes*, in which he describes his theory of insight learning and becomes a major proponent of the Gestalt school of psychology.

▷ 1929

Edwin G. Boring

Publishes influential *A History of Experimental Psychology*.

▷ 1932

Jean Piaget

Publishes *The Moral Judgement of the Child* and later becomes a very important figure in child development and cognitive psychology.

▷ 1937

Gordon Allport

Publishes *Personality: A Psychological Interpretation*, and is considered the father of modern personality theory.

▷ 1954

Abraham Maslow

Helps found the school of humanistic psychology and later develops an influential theory of motivation.

▷ 1954

Kenneth B. Clark

Research with his wife Mamie is cited by the U.S. Supreme Court in a decision to overturn racial discrimination in schools. He later becomes the first African American president of the American Psychological Association.

▷ 1957

Leon Festinger

Develops what many consider the most important and comprehensive theory in social psychology—the theory of cognitive dissonance.

▷ 1958

Herbert Simon

Presents his views on information processing theory and later receives the Nobel Prize for his research on cognition.

▷ 1965

Stanley Milgram

Conducts highly controversial study of obedience and disobedience to authority, which many consider the most famous single study in psychology.

▷ 1970

Mary Ainsworth

Demonstrates the importance of attachment in the social development of children.

▷ 1980

David Hubel & Torsten Wiesel

Win the Nobel Prize for their work identifying cortical cells that respond to specific events in the visual field.

▷ 1987

Anne Anastasi

Author of the classic text on psychological testing, as well as numerous articles on psychological testing and assessment and is awarded the National Medal of Science.

Please note that due to space limitations we could not include most contemporary psychologists, as well as many psychologists who have made significant contributions to psychology.

▷ 1891

Mary Whiton Calkins

Establishes a psychology laboratory at Wellesley and later becomes the first woman president of the American Psychology Association.

▷ 1892

Edward Titchener

Earns his doctorate and moves to the United States, where he continues his work with the structuralist technique of introspective analysis at Cornell.

▷ 1894

Margaret Floy Washburn

First woman to receive a Ph.D. in psychology and later writes several important textbooks on comparative psychology.

▷ 1898

Edward Thorndike

One of the pioneers in animal learning who develops the "law of effect" as a result of research on trial and error learning of animals using his puzzle box.

▷ 1914

Carl Jung

Splits with Freud and forms an offshoot of psychoanalysis called analytical psychology.

▷ 1916

Leta Stetter-Hollingsworth

Receives her Ph.D. and goes on to publish the first works on the psychology of women.

▷ 1920

Francis Cecil Sumner

First African American to receive a Ph.D. in psychology and later founded one of America's leading psychology departments.

▷ 1924

Mary Cover Jones

Demonstrates how to use conditioning to remove a child's fear, and is credited by some with pioneering behavior therapy.

▷ 1938

B.F. Skinner

Publishes *Behavior of Organisms*, helps found behaviorism, and later becomes one of the most prominent psychologists of the 20th century.

▷ 1942

Carl Rogers

Publishes *Counseling and Psychotherapy*, and later becomes an important figure in modern clinical and humanistic psychology.

▷ 1946

Solomon Asch

Demonstrates crucial factors in impression formation and later studies the effects of group pressure on independence and conformity.

▷ 1950

Erik Erikson

Publishes *Childhood and Society*, which revises Freud's psychoanalytic theory and extends it across the life span.

▷ 1961

John Berry

Presents his ideas on the importance of cross-cultural research in psychology.

▷ 1963

Albert Bandura

Along with Richard Walters, writes *Social Learning and Personality Development*, in which he describes the effects of observational learning on personality development.

▷ 1963

Lawrence Kohlberg

Demonstrates the sequence of moral development.

▷ 1964

Roger Sperry

Publishes his split-brain research. Later receives the Nobel Prize for his work.

▷ 1992

Eleanor Gibson

Awarded the National Medal of Science for her lifetime of research on topics such as depth perception and basic processes involved with reading.